Putting the "Pre" in Appreciation

TAMMY JOY LANE

NEWMAN SPRINGS PUBLISHING
320 Broad Street
Red Bank, NJ 07701

First originally published by Newman Springs Publishing 2019

ISBN 978-1-64096-757-1 (Paperback)
ISBN 978-1-64096-758-8 (Digital)

Printed in the United States of America

To everyone who believed in me until I could believe in myself

There are empty pages at the end to write down people you want to appreciate before they die, or ideas that come while you are reading this. Those blank pages and the people and ideas you write on them will be the most valuable part of this book.

THANK YOU IN ADVANCE #TYIA

. . . .

It would be super weird if I wrote a book about putting the "pre" in appreciation and didn't start out for thanking *you* for reading this. I mean, seriously, there are nearly 130 million books that have been published, or as I am writing this my highly researched Google goddess told me that there are 129,864,880 published books to be exact.

There are more-than-I-can-count titles on Netflix, I promise; I called them, you can call too if you want. It's 1-866-579-7172, oh, wait I'm on hold, he is looking for a more exact number. My commitment to research should ease your mind on the validity of this book. Jaren, employee at Netflix, you rock, thanks for your help in my extensive research!

There are so many things these days competing for our time, money, and attention that I know it can be at times overwhelming. PTA turned PTO, jobs, family activities, Girl Scouts, Boy Scouts, football in the fall, basketball/volleyball in the winter, baseball in the spring, dancing lessons on Monday, gymnastics on Thursdays, church meetings, volunteering, Rotary, fake book clubs, I could go on and on forever naming all the things that pull and push us, light us on fire, and burn us out. So the chance of *you* picking up this book is one in three million…so, thank you, I appreciate you. You matter. Reading good crap matters.

If you actually make it to the end, you can bet on even another thank-you because I know how precious time is, how precious *your* time is. So, thank you, thank you in advance; thank you for being here with me.

Hopefully we can shift from a *high-expectation/low-appreciation* world to a world of grateful wonder. A world where we treat each other like we matter.

Realizing that the struggle is real some days and even getting up out of bed takes an act of God or Grace or whatever you believe in.

Creating a world where we acknowledge that we don't know the entire story of why people are the way they are. Over 6,000 people die every hour, so if at least five people are affected by that then that means every hour 30,000 people are walking around with the knowledge that they just lost their sister, their husband, their mom, or their child.

Talking about life-altering, take-your-breath-away situations, on that note there are nearly 2,400 divorces a day. Multiply by two for both parties affected, add in the 2.5 kids per household, and not to mention the people in the neighborhood, extended family, or other areas affected and that is a whopping 10,800 people a day trying to put on a smile and act like everything is fine even though their life as they know it will never be the same.

Remember this line: *We don't know what people are hiding behind their smile or their scowl.* We don't know what take-your-breath-away, stop-your-heart, life-changing event happened right before someone crosses our path. *Pause,* breathe; it's not always about you. Be kinder than you feel people deserve. Let people be human. Let's join together to make it #safetobehuman. There is an amazing TedxTalk my friend Karen Eddington gave, check it out. Pause, set this book down and watch it; seriously, it's good stuff. Don't add it to your to-do-later list; there is no later, there is only now.

Use this link (https://youtu.be/JPnH-OY0DaM) or search YouTube for Karen Eddington TedxIdahoFalls 2017.

Something has to change. I think its best instead of complaining about the price of gas, or the government, or construction on 1-15 we must take responsibility for our own thoughts/words/actions and how they affect the world as a whole. I know that as we use the power of preappreciation, gratitude and thankfulness we can shift the world to a kinder, more loving, safe place to be.

Special thanks to Stephanie Staples, Tannen-Ellis Graham and the entire crew at TedxIdahoFalls; without them this book would not even be in your hand right now. Stephanie, for finding me in the elevator and giving breath to this idea, helping me see that my idea was worth sharing. To Tannen, for pushing me to up my game, to align my words with my actions and inspiring me to be more than I was. You are changing the world my friend. TedxIdahoFalls thank you, all of you, for showing up and creating a space for people to make a change and shift the world. All of it matters. You matter.

To my three girls, Brooklyn, Liberty, and Isabell, who loved me even when I act unlovable and unkind, who taught me to forgive fast and to love easy. I'm trying to stop yelling, I promise.

To my family who loved me through hell, who tolerated me when I was intolerable, who visited me in the psych wards, who send me mail while deployed in Iraq, who loved me through it all even when it must have been so hard. To my mom and dad, for teaching me to spell "fun" as W-O-R-K.

To Mike. For funding my kindness business over and over again, for giving me the space and freedom to be who I needed to be. For being the mom to the kids so I could always go when I needed to. And to so many more, I could write an entire book on all the people I am grateful for, so if you aren't named here, know that your contribution to my life is no less important. I see you.

CHAPTER ONE

. . . .

Save a Life

Preappreciation has the power to save lives. Because it saved mine. When I was little, I wanted to grow up and be like Mother Teresa: I wanted to travel the world and really make it a better place. After so many dreams turned into nightmares, I had given up, and my new dream was, "I hope I don't wake up tomorrow," and when people would die, I would have severe death envy. You see, I found myself at a fork in the road: this way was shit and that way was shittier. And I literally didn't know which was which.

I had this dream to buy a motorhome and travel America spreading kindness. Problem was, shortly after my family of five moved into the motorhome, we realized that we did not like each other enough to be in such close quarters. I ended up in a trailer park, and my husband went to his parents; neither one of us were compromising.

I had the kids during the day and he had them at night, so as I sat alone in the trailer park, surrounded by my thirty-four-foot failure, I felt like I couldn't breathe. I felt like literally I could implode from the inside out.

I lived relatively close to Colorado, so I thought maybe I could just take a trip there and become fluent in marijuana. I had friends who drank every weekend, I could maybe try that. But luckily, I looked around my motorhome and I found a stack of 4x6 cards— you know the ones that you used to use as flash cards in junior high school. My dad taught me to keep them on hand in case I had a good idea…believe me I did not write down any of my ideas.

I started writing thank-you cards to anyone I could think of: old bosses, people at the grocery store, the lady in church who plays the organ, my family, my estranged husband (although I didn't put a stamp on his…and he still got it!).

If I had a name and an address, they were getting a postcard! I would write thank-you cards until I fell asleep or until I felt better, and the thing I found was when I looked for the good in others, I could see the good in myself. I am not the same person today as I was just a few years ago. When I meet new people now, I forget that they will never know the girl whose main focus in life was to find the fastest way to die, and failed, and failed, and failed. Thank God that I did! I could never see the light at the end of the tunnel. I could not see past my beating myself up, past my putting myself down, past my past, or past the train of people I had hurt along my way. I couldn't get out of bed, I couldn't answer the phone, I couldn't even breathe.

Because you bought this book, I am going to mail you two cards: one is for you, because I know how hard it is to read a book these days, and the other one is blank and that is for you to send to someone who has made a difference in your life. Why do we wait for someone's funeral to tell them that they have made a difference in our life? Somewhere along the way, someone decided that we should wait to say thank you—don't wait! Preappreciate with me, join me in making people feel like it matters that they are here. Because it does, it matters that you are still here.

(To receive the two cards in the mail follow this link https://form.jotform.com/TammyjoyLane/preappreciation)

CHAPTER TWO

. . . .

The Beginning

It all started with a business trip. The kind of business trip that you know you definitely shouldn't go on because your kindness business isn't actually making any money. You know, the one where you are sharing the hotel room with practically a stranger, you packed in your suitcase a full box of cereal…and milk—just kidding on the milk!

The business trip where you are mostly going to get out of the house because if one more person calls you mom, or needs you to wipe their butt you just might actually lose your sh——.

The business trip where your kid was throwing up all night before, so you literally got thirty minutes of sleep before you had to leave your sick baby, wondering if you're going to mom hell because if you stay your soul will die possibly to the point of no recovery and if you go you might just hear something that will change your life.

So, I went, on no sleep, no cash, on credit cards that were close to being maxed out, and a prayer, a prayer of *Please God, let me hear something that will change my life.* Something that would help me turn my kindness business into an actual non-money pit—maybe even just to break even, maybe?

I went against all odds, against my better judgment, and with an overwhelming load of mom guilt. When I met my new friend/ hotel partner to carpool to the airport, she complained the entire way about how she only got four hours of sleep. In that moment, I realized the things we complain about are the same things those around us would *kill* for! I'm not perfect at it yet, but I promised myself I would do better at being grateful and minimize my complaining… easier said than done. We have so much to be grateful for, yet we can't even see it because we complain like it's our job.

When you want to complain, flip it to gratitude. It is 2019 for heck's sake! If you are complaining about something then you know there is a possibility for it to be dif-

ferent! (I heard this at the Jack Canfield Event called "One Day to Greatness." Pause now and go register for a life-changing event at jackcanfield.com.)

**Preappreciation
Pre-Step
Minimize Complaining**

So do it! Change it! Trade it! Swap it! Stop it! Go there! Be who you know you can be, or if not then at least be quiet!

The world is so full of negativity and complaining will just perpetuate the problem. Start using your words for good to create the life you want! You have more power than you are using…well, actually you probably are using your power—you just need to shift it from "not effective" to "effective" creation.

I used to worry about a flooding basement. I'm not sure where it came from, but I would literally say, "A basement flood would be the worst thing ever." I would dream about it, I would talk about my dreams, and create more and more worry feelings around a flooding basement.

One day, I started a bath for our daughter and forgot; I forgot for a long time. The basement flooded good… I'm talking down the floor vent, walls, sheetrock, carpet, a whole big mess. If that wasn't enough to show me how powerful of a worry creator I was being, another flood happened while this one was still being repaired. The kitchen sink leaked through the floor, through the basement ceiling, right into my office that held all of my most important things and ideas. I lost garbage bags full of very important junk of which, to this day, none I can remember.

So good experience, right? Instead of being pissed off, I chose to be grateful for the experience and think of all the business it brought to the contractor of both jobs; I didn't let it take me out. Little did I know I had one more gut-wrenching punch coming to reinforce the power of creation that worry has.

I had split up with my husband for the millionth time. I bought my own house—my credit score used to be 420 back in 2006 so this was a huge accomplishment for me. I was trying to save money, so I decided to cut out the inspection…of a 1940 house. Hmmmm, not my best decision ever, anyway the very day I signed the papers and moved in, the entire basement flooded—I'm talking several inches of water, a borrowed sump pump, neighbors-and-friends-to-the-rescue kind of a flood…and it was January, in Utah, which wasn't that cold actually, considering at the moment I am writing this I am in upstate New York, which gives me a greater appreciation for Utah cold.

This flood turned into a total gut job, and still to this day it has not been fixed. Thank goodness my renter is flexible and easy going. I'm just waiting for this book to make the top-seller list, so I can go back and fix that basement up…LOL…not kidding.

I finally got the message. I am a creator. Up to this point in my life I was what we call a crap creator…taking all my worries and turning them into exactly the life *I didn't want*! I could go on and on about this crappy creation, but I'm sure you get the point and now you are looking back at your life thinking about all the times you used your powers to create a crap life. Good news… *We can change.*

Focus.

Okay.

Apparently, focus is one of the major obstacles of this book, so just prepare to laugh with me, I'm only human. It's okay to be human.

Okay. So, back to the Business Trip Story.

So, at the conference, which was amazing and powerful and wonderful, I met my friend there, her name is Karen Jacobsen. She is known as the GPS Girl, she was the original voice in the Australian

GPS Systems and is now a powerful, wonderful musician and motivational speaker who helps people and businesses "recalculate". If you are needing a boost in your life or company, you have got to have her at your next event! Find her at thegpsgirl.com. She sat down with me and helped me decide on yestokindness.com instead of what I had originally planned on: "ConsciousKindness"—who the heck can spell conscious anyway?

Well, at the end of the conference I had my bags all packed, ready to go to the curb. Usually, I would handle it like a boss and take the bags to the curb by myself, like the strong, independent woman that I am, but I'm learning that it's okay to ask for help.

I called the front desk. As I waited for the bellman to come up, I reached into my purse and I grabbed a five-dollar bill. I wanted to avoid that awkward ending where I would have to flip through my hundreds to find a $1 bill to give him. (Joking, I definitely didn't have 100's but you know what I'm talking about. I know you have been a waitress or something where someone has opened their wallet and done that.)

Well, when he came to the door, I could see on his face that he was less than thrilled with his life. A lot like my own, and maybe even you reading this, his life maybe hadn't turned out as he had planned.

A voice came to my head, it said, "Give him the money now." You know some people call that inspiration, other people call it psychosis, and because I have previous experience with this voice, I knew not to argue. I handed him the money.

I will never forget how his whole face lit up. Instead of just getting my bags, dropping them at the curb, and moving on, he was really there with me. He started asking who I was, where I was from, and why I was this way. By the time we reached the front desk, I had learned about him, where he was from, how he ended up here, and we became great friends. We would still be friends today if I didn't have a propensity to change my phone number two or three times a year. Sometimes, when I can't change anything else, just for changing's sake I will change my phone number, or dinner table, or husband—I have had a lot of different dinner tables.

He gave me a voucher for breakfast and drinks for me and my friend. He was telling all his coworkers about me like I was a hero. I had simply changed the timing of something I was going to do anyway. This changed the entire outcome of the experience; it created a space for a connection because I showed appreciation before instead of after.

This is my first experience with preappreciation, and I couldn't wait to find other ways to use it!

CHAPTER THREE

....

The Magic of Jimmy John's

In 2016-ish I was living in South Ogden, Utah, the same house that flooded the day I moved in. Because it was a total gut job, I wanted to put in a new HVAC system while the walls were open, so I needed a bid. I have friends who do bids for people, plumbers, electricians, HVAC people, so I know that the time they would be spending with me would be free for me, yay. I should be grateful, but all I could think about during that time he wouldn't be making any money for his family.

I wanted to find a way to appreciate him in a way that would really matter. I know their days are long and packed full, so I decided to order a Jimmy John's sandwich. I had it delivered a few minutes before he arrived, when he came to the door I handed it to him.

I said, "I know days are busy, so I just wanted to say thank you in advance." Soooo, after he got over the initial shock of it all—he was totally weirded out momentarily—he genuinely thanked me, and instead of showing up giving me an overpriced bid and moving on, he sat down with me and we came up with a mutually beneficial arrangement.

I have had so many bids before where they come in, treat you like a number, and you can tell they can't wait to get out of there and on to the next bid. Truth is, we never know what is going on in someone's life if they come into our house or life and give us less than perfect service. They could be one of the people affected by losing someone to death, or suicide, divorce, or many other options of things that make for a crappy day.

Jimmy John's is the most underutilized form of service. Think about it for a minute, you can make a phone call or order online at jimmyjohns.com and someone will drop off a sandwich for you. And they are really, really good sandwiches with gluten-free options. So try it; set down the book and send someone a sandwich. If you want to make a real difference in someone's life, try it. Or if you're hangry right now—you know, when hungry and angry have a baby—then do the whole world a service and order a sandwich for yourself so you can be easier to love. Hangry is a real thing, and it is way harder to be kind if you are starving and irritable.

My husband, for a long time, worked as a service advisor at a dealership. Real quick, let me tell you how to put the pre in appreciation for them. First off, we must stop asking people to work for free. Imagine if you worked as a teller at a bank, and a customer came in and asked for some help, but before you helped them they asked you to clock out and process their transaction for free. This wouldn't happen, right? It would be absurd if we expected this or even asked for it. But we do this all the damn time when we go to a car dealership and ask for a free diagnostic, free. Free. Free. Free for you means someone has to work an hour without getting paid; it means more pressure, more stress, more, more, more...what? All of this so you can get a free diagnostic? Think about things before you expect anything, and if there is a situation where you are going to ask for a discount or free, then show a little appreciation before you ask someone to work for free.

I used to take my car to Young Chrysler Jeep Dodge in Morgan, Utah. The first time I went there I took a dozen donuts, not because I was going to ask for anything free or because I wanted something, but just because I know from living with someone who has had that job that it is hard.

They were so grateful. Every time I went there after that I felt like they were always happy to see me. I felt like as a customer, I made a difference. I didn't always take donuts, but if I could I would because it feels good to put the pre in appreciation. Honestly, business is hard these days, people are so freaking needy and they want more and more and want to give less and less. Customers actually kind of suck. I hope you are not one of crappy ones, but if you are, then please figure it out. Take my course on kindness and realize that your high-expectation entitled ass is causing a lot of stress, and some-day companies won't even want you as a customer.

And please for the love of everything if you are a business owner, please teach your people how to acknowledge people when they come in your door. Even if you're with a customer, look up, *smile*, say, "I'll be right with you." It is so hard to spend money on things you really don't want to be spending your money on...so make it easy for people to spend money with you by appreciating the fact that they even came in your door. A smile is a simple way to put the pre in appreciation.

One time I went into a dealership with a dozen donuts, liter-ally no one said *hello, hi, be there in a minute*, nothing. For a long while—and this is a big dealership. I went somewhere else and never came back. By not acknowledging people, you lose good customers.

I don't care what is going on, when someone comes to your house, say hello. Welcome them. Pause, acknowledge their existence. People know you can't always stop what you're doing to help them right away, but acknowledge.

The good thing about being married four times and having eight sisters is that you can say things in a book and not specify which family or which sister it was so no one can get too mad.

Well, one of my four different families I mar-ried into I never quite got along with, and one of the main reasons on my end was that whenever I showed up, no one said anything, not hello, not hi, nothing. I would even say hi, and they

Acknowledgement is one of the best ways to show appreciation

would ignore me. I thought this was so strange; I thought something was wrong with me. It probably wouldn't have been so bad, but I came from a mom that welcomed people in at the door, and when they left she walked them to the door.

It didn't matter who you were or why you were there, she was going to greet you with a smile and make sure you say a good goodbye. On many occasions—well, I guess just once because I learn fast—I got "in trouble" for sneaking out of the house, and by this I mean leaving the party without saying goodbye. If you come for dinner, you will see, she is the best! Love you, Mom.

If you don't take anything away from this book, take this: Start to acknowledge people that come into your house, your work, your life. It is amazing what happens when you open yourself up to connection by acknowledging people.

I do not believe that anything is an accident; I truly believe that people come into our life to teach us how to be, and some come into our life to teach us how *not* to be. Sometimes we act in ways that inspire others to be better, do better, and live better. The flip side is also true, at times we are the ones who teach others how not to be. We're all just humans here doing human things, and sometimes it works and sometimes it doesn't.

We have to find a way to let ourselves and the people around us be human, imperfect, and beautiful flaws and all. We have got to shut off our autocorrect and just let people be comfortable around us. It's okay. You're okay, I'm okay. Let's just be human kind...want to?

CHAPTER FOUR

· ·

The Uber Rider Reset

The next time this happened to me was quite by chance. You know, when you have a kindness business you have to have a lot of side jobs, so as one of them I am a hot Uber driver. It is the craziest job, you never know what you are going to get. And in case you are wondering, we talk about you when you get out of the car; there is an entire private Facebook page where we discuss professionally (LOL) the ridiculousness that happens in our cars.

One night, four drunk people get into my car, the same car that my babies sit in and throw Cheerios all over, that I have to vacuum out before I can "go online." So they get in, I throw my head back and roll my eyes and thought, "this is going to be a long ride." I couldn't wait for them to get out of my car.

Miraculously, when the last guy got into the front seat, he reached over and handed me a twenty dollar bill, and what that did for me is that it *reset* all the past drunk-guy experiences that I was carrying with me and judging them. I let them go and could just be there with them, appreciating their drunk selves.

Wouldn't it have been so horrible if he had given me that twenty at the end, and then I would have had to feel guilty for being a jerk the entire time? You see we never know what people are carrying, or why they are the way they are. When we show up and get bad service we are usually being treated based on the bad experience of the previous crappy customers.

Preappreciation can bring that person right here with you and helps them let go of the past bad experiences. We have so much power to make someone's day and remind them that their service matters. How we treat people matters. We the People, the people in the service industry, are here to serve; we are not your servants, and we have to stop acting like we are above or better than those who serve us.

Try this next time you go to a restaurant, flip through your hundreds or ones and find a five dollar bill. Hand it to your server, pause, and look them in the eyes and say, "Thank you for showing up today, it matters that you are here." Let the fact that they are showing up for you be enough, let go of your expectation and high demands and let someone be enough.

Be easy to serve. If you know you are high maintenance then that is okay, give them a twenty up front and you can be as high maintenance as you want. Seriously people, what is happening to our world? We expect so much and give so little, why are we this way?

Leave a trail of goodness behind you, be the customer that people smile because you walk in the door, not the one who makes everyone cringe. Honestly, life is hard for everyone, it's all different, but we have the power to be the light in someone's life, so do it.

I have had waitresses cry when I handed them a tip in advance, I have had Uber drivers open up and share their hopes and dreams because I gave them a tip in advance. Connection after connection after connection because I choose to look at people not as a transaction but as real people, with real struggles, with real hopes and dreams that they have given up on.

I hope you have not given up on yours, but if you have, then start preappreciating people like it's your job, and your entire world will open up. Put your phone down, look up, notice people, say hi, smile, compliment, and you will meet people that will rock your world. I'm not kidding.

Just yesterday I was at Dollar Tree and the person behind me in line had a few things in her hand, so I said, "Hi, let me buy your stuff for you." She was a little shocked but then thankfully let me. We got to talking, and she runs this organization in town, and I don't know what will come of it, but the right people are all around us, we are just missing them. We miss the connection because we are looking for a transaction. Stop it. Stop looking at people in a how-can-I-benefit-from-talking-to-them kind of a way. Just show up, acknowledge people, love people, find out what they are hiding behind their smile or their scowl and then serve them or connect them to someone who can change their world.

Seriously, I am having lunch with a board member from NAMI on Friday because while I was at the DMV getting my driver's license, instead of complaining—well, actually I think we did complain a little together, but—we started talking and became friends. I was thinking back about all that it took for the two of us to be in line together, and it was surely a divine appointment that the two of us were supposed to meet.

I had shown up earlier that day and had to go home for more paperwork, and then I had my husband's card so the lady told me to go across the street to the ATM. And then I still didn't have the right paperwork so she sent me down the hall to get my voter registration card, so I could have been so upset and steaming mad that it took all day, but instead I looked around with grateful wonder and got to meet someone very great. Check out her website and order some of her artwork (fineartamerica.com, Terry Boulerice). Oh! And I forgot to mention that she was in the wrong line anyway, when she got her turn at the desk she told her to go to another line…so, seriously the people who you need to connect with are all around you!

You see, the world is trying to put together people who can do the most good, problem is to many of us are busy complaining and replaying and recomplaining and even one-up complaining, that we can't even pause to see what blessings are trying to come into our life.

CHAPTER FIVE

· ·

Exchange Complaining with Complimenting

Okay, this chapter is the most important one, I think the entire book could be about my experience with this, but I'm going to wrap it up into one chapter. So, listen to me just for a minute, don't worry about this weekend, what happened last week, or what you're going to say to the lady at work that stresses you out, just be here with me now for a second.

There is this thing we don't do very well anymore, and the good news is that it is simple and easy to change. The thing we don't do is look for the good. We are all so busy pointing out what is wrong and giving advice on how it can be better that we can't even be present enough to appreciate the majesty of things going on right in front of our eyes.

If a flight gets delayed, we spend the time complaining, posting negativity on social media, or royally freaking out inside because life isn't going exactly as we planned. I used to be this way, so I know you can change too.

This is how I act when a plane gets delayed: I look around and find someone I am supposed to meet, I look at myself as a powerful force that can shut down entire airports if that is what needs to happen to meet the perfect people.

So, I plan a trip to visit my sister, I align a babysitter… I have a babysitter, someone is going to watch my kids for me, while I go away for the weekend by myself. So, I get a ride from Logan, Utah to Salt Lake City, Utah, it's about an hour and a half, plus or minus. My friend packs up her two kids and drives me there, I have the best friends ever. Thanks, Michelle. So, we arrive a little early and I think this was sometime in February or March…maybe even April. I don't remember it being prime storm time.

So, I go into the airport and its crazy busy, and I can see people are in a panic, not like in-danger panic but that blank stare of are-you-kidding-me now-what-am-I-supposed-to-do-now-that-my-life-plan-has-been-derailed kind of a panic. The vibes in there were out-of-control, stressed-out chaotic. I walk up to the check-in desk and the agent informs me that my flight has been cancelled—not rescheduled, not delayed, cancelled. Cancelled.

I look at the lady like, what the hell… I have a babysitter, I can't just go home. I literally wanted to cry: not like a poor-me kind of cry, but an Oh-my—hell, I have a babysitter and a trip and seriously I can't go home. There were literally no options to get me there—oh wait, there was one, like four days later. I don't have a babysitter in four days, I have one right now!

After I realized that there was nothing to do, no flights, no backup plans, no one really cared about my babysitter, there was a storm in Denver that literally shut down the entire airport. There were obviously a lot bigger issues for a ton of people, but to me, this was soul crushing.

I looked around and saw people around me, shocked, crying, frantic. I took a deep breath. I saw a lady sitting on the chairs; there was an open chair next to her. I sat down and asked her where she was supposed to be flying to. She had flown in from Pennsylvania to Denver; she wasn't even supposed to be in Salt Lake City. They had rerouted her entire plane, so that we could be at that moment and meet. To this day, Kathy is a very good friend; whenever we are in the same city we meet up and my life is fully enriched because I calmed down, looked around, and noticed those around me.

I ended up asking her if she wanted to sleep over at my house! I was sure she was going to say no, ya know, since we just met and because I was a complete stranger. She said YES! My friend turned around and came back and picked us up. We drove up to Ogden, Utah and I gave her a tour of the town, told her about the Mormons— you can find out more at comeuntochrist.org. It was hilarious and fun, and crazy, and so so life changing. My house was an hour from the airport, so she ended up getting a hotel close to the airport and invited me to stay with her. I'll never forget when she called her husband and told him she got invited to sleep over at my house.

Life can be a fun crazy adventure if we just calm the frick down. Life isn't always going to go as planned; we cram our lives so so so full and leave no room for anyone in our lives to be human. Including the people we do business with.

Next time your plane is delayed, or your driver is late, or your friend ditches you—just look around and see what you need to do instead. See who you are supposed to meet, stop complaining and just freaking be excited that something amazing is about to happen.

I have made so many friends over the past few years because I traded out complimenting for complaining. I'm not kidding. It's amazing, and you can too. If meeting new people and making real connections isn't your thing, don't worry, there is a chapter later on about how to appreciate an introvert. Stay with me here. (Just kidding, there is no chapter on that. I would have no clue what to write.)

If you think meeting people is hard, try this…everyone you come into contact with, I'm talking within a five-foot radius: compliment them. Here are some examples:

"I love your hair."

"You look great in that color."

"I like your shirt."

I'm serious. We try to overcomplicate things, and then don't do them because we can't find a soul-level compliment. Screw that! People spend a lot of money on their hair! Notice it! So many people have said, "You just made my week." Seriously…why in the hell are we living in a world where a compliment from a stranger is the best thing that has happened to you?

So, you see the power in a compliment is so so so important, it's not always about the shirt or the hair, it's the fact that someone crossed your path and your phone was out of your hand, you looked them in the eyes, found something good about them, and let them know.

One time in the gym I told this lady, "I love your hair," and she replied, "Thanks, it's fake." We both smiled. I of course went on to think about how often we compare our real to other people's fake. There is so much fakeness going on these days; the world is dying for someone to be real, to be here, to see them. Be that person. Be that person that lets your phone die sometimes, so you can see the people around you before they die.

Be that person who in a world where you can find anything, you find the good. Be the person that in a world where you can be anything, be the good. Be that person that in a world where you can see anything, see the good. This brings me to this awesome Facebook group called BE THE GOOD. My friend Christa Perschon Lysager started it as a place to share good things you do, see, or happen to you. She will send free BE THE GOOD stickers to anyone for free; she even pays the shipping. Once a month she sells T-shirts and hoodies that say "BE THE GOOD" so she can curb the cost of the stickers. This is the thing, the difference you can make if you just start, drop perfection, and just be. Pause, find the group, join it! (https://www.facebook.com/groups/939831162810379/)

I actually sent my friend a text today, we had met for a meeting and she had a beautiful red jacket on. In the text I said, "You look amazing in red," to which she replied, "Thank you I really needed that compliment today." Who knows what is going on in her life, who knows what is going on in anyone's life?

Try this! With your kids, compliment to connect before you correct

Sometimes even the people we live with, we have no idea of the struggles that they face every day. We have to do a better job at making it #safetobehuman and complimenting others is a big step in the right direction.

Try it. The five-foot rule. Don't be discouraged if someone ignores you, it might mean they have earbuds in. Don't get discouraged, and don't expect to always get a positive response; some people only get compliments when someone wants something, so be flexible and don't give up. Share your experience with me! (preappreciation@gmail.com) I love to hear about how things go. I'm not just making up a bunch of stuff I think would be a good idea, I have actually tried this and my life is so much better because of it. And yours can be too!

CHAPTER SIX

· ·

Take the Ass out of Association

Let's talk association meetings. I know several of you reading this are probably a member of an association. I currently am a member of two different amazing ones, but over the years I have tried or visited all different types of associations or groups.

Junior high called, they want their tactics back. Some associations that are currently in process need to get themselves in check. Backbiting. Gossip. Drama. Judging. Selective welcoming, etc. has got to stop.

Recently, I joined a group and the way I showed up really apparently turned some people off, and they didn't like how I just showed up uninvited. Others were impressed with my bravery and initiative for just showing up and saying "hey, I want to join." The point is, if you get out of bed in the morning, then your chances of pissing someone off are very high. Especially these days when people are just looking for someone to blame for their unhappiness. Don't get wrapped up in it…just do your thing and spend time around those who see your greatness and let those who don't do their thing without falling into their drama.

I just gave a new member talk at one of my clubs. I thought it was so good, I'm just going to type it right up here in this chapter. A big thanks to Bob Kittell, an internationally renowned award-winning speaker and friend of mine who taught me to give every speech like it was my last. Check out his site, he has some really great online training courses for memory (www.bobkittell.com).

New Member Speech for Rotary International September 2017

Someone once told me to give every talk like it was my last, so if I only had three minutes I wouldn't spend it thanking my sponsor, just kidding, thanks John for sponsoring me. I wouldn't spend the time telling you about how I grew up in a middle-class family of ten kids, in Utah. I would remind you that many hands make light work and if we all do a little the burden doesn't fall upon a few. I wouldn't spend my three minutes talking about the time that I joined the army because I was in love with a boy, and when I went home and asked my dad if he thought it was a good idea - this was October 2001, so of course he said no, he thought it was a horrible idea, to which I replied…tooooo late!

I spent the next several years trying to convince him and everyone else that I joined the army to serve my country, but we all know that it's that power of love that makes us do crazy things, and at this time in life when discrimination and destruction are taking over its that Love that we need to pull us back together and make the world #safetobehuman.

I wouldn't spend my three minutes talking about the time when after I returned from Iraq, and I wasn't transitioning into "real" life, sitting on the edge of a mountain with my own life in my hands. I would remind you that and the physical and emotional energy it takes to even show up to an event like this is sometimes overwhelming, and you never know what people are hiding behind their smile or their scowl, so as community and business leaders and fellow Rotarians, what else is our purpose if not to make life easier for others.

The End.

A few people told me that it was the best new member talk they had ever heard, and it was under three minutes. What I'm saying is that we sometimes forget that the point of an association or a club or a membership is to lift each other up, to bring us together to be better than we can on our own.

Rotary International is great club where you can really make a difference—check it out! (www.rotary.org) *then ask someone in the local club to invite you to go with them!

It's not about who is president, or who can be better than who. We have lost it; we seriously have been emphasizing the "ass" in association. Let's take that out. Want to?

Welcome people, smile, show up early, stay late, volunteer to help where you can, and if you can't then contribute in other ways, like money or good attitude. Please, please I beg of you stop complaining about this and that, make a change or be quiet. Stop draining those around you by finding what is wrong, if it bugs you that bad then do something about it.

What the crap does this have to do about putting the "pre" in appreciation you may be wondering? Well, the past two years I have been going to what is called the National Speakers Association. Every month at the local meeting in Utah we would have a guest speaker. One day I thought, hmm, what if I send a thank-you note to this guy before he comes to Utah? He was coming from California and they donate their time, so I thought it would make him smile knowing he was appreciated just for showing up. The very first month, the guest speaker came up to me and gave me a *hug*! It was so cool. His name was Jeffery; I will never forget this experience.

I tried to do it every time, by mail, but sometimes that didn't pan out, so I would even do an e-mail the morning of. I moved to upstate New York in March of 2017, but my mom and dad still go to the NSA Chapter in Utah, so one month I e-mailed the guest speaker who happened to be the President of NSA that year, Dr. John Molidor. He replied that he had seen a lot of things over the years, but he was going to always remember that and take it with him.

I promise it works. People love it. They love to be appreciated any time, but there is something special about taking the time to do it before. It takes more effort and a little bit of research, but it's so worth it.

Once a year there is an event called "Influence," if you haven't been, go register now (nsaspeaker.org). I promise your life will never be the same! There is a section there to say who referred you, put my name there, LOL…not joking. I could win a contest…anyway, it is the event of the year. Speakers come from all over the world to be trained, inspired, and meet together. I thought to myself, that this is probably the most stressful speaking engagement ever because, not to be judgmental but, speakers are super judgmental of other speakers. They are either thinking, "Why did they choose them to speak, I could do a way better job" or they're critiquing every tiny bit of body language, every word, every wrong breath, and will go up and tell them after they are done.

So, I thought wouldn't it be nice to get a thank-you in advance, a word of encouragement from a fellow speaker? I promise you, if you do this, people will *love you*.

The schedule is always published before the event, and you can easily find their address to mail them a hand-written postcard before they speak. The first year I did this, I ran out of time so in the end I just e-mailed the ones I didn't have time to mail cards to. The response was the same; it doesn't matter how you preappreciate people, *just do it*!

Sometimes we get so wrapped up in doing the perfect thing that we end up doing nothing. The entire ironic thing about me writing a book about showing appreciation is that I have had four weddings, and I never once sent any thank-you notes for all the gifts. I just want to take a moment here to thank everyone who has come to my weddings and given me gifts, over and over and over and one more over again. Thank you.

So, the good news is that people can change. Use this idea, even if you just send them to the speakers that you look up or want to see; wouldn't it be great if you were speaking at an event and you got a thank-you note from a few of your fans before the event? I'm just saying seriously, try this, use all these ideas, and make them better, then tell me about it. E-mail me anytime (preappreciation@gmail.com) or leave a note through my website at yestokindness.com.

This is the benefit of putting the "pre" in appreciation when it comes to conferences, breakout sessions, yearly events, etc.: it lets you make a connection with the people who you admire *before* the conference. The past two years I have had a list of people who had told me to find them when I got to the conference because of a simple postcard sent before the event.

There is another thing that happened that I didn't see coming. I almost didn't go to the event this year—like I say, I have a kindness business so sometimes that means a lot of outgoing and not so much incoming. Literally, I didn't have enough money to attend. I had already purchased my flight, but I did not have money for the cost of the conference or hotel or food. I told my friend that I was not going to attend, and I went home to lay in my bed, depressed. I got a message that day from Lea Woodford, CEO and founder of the SmartFem Media Group (SmartFem.com). She had received my card and wanted to meet me at the conference... HOW COULD I NOT GO? Royalty was requesting my introduction!

This little thing of sending thank-you cards ended up changing the trajectory of my life. I went. I didn't pay any of my bills that month. I asked my favorite roommate in the world, (Tannen-Ellis Graham, an amazing speaker, coach and branding expert, find her at careerkarma360.com), if we could have extra roommates so it would be cheaper. I showed up, I met people, I listened to people, I took a risk, I showed up because someone on the day I was going to give up and just be miserable, messaged me, and said, please find me at the conference.

I'm saying you never know what it takes for people to show up. You never know why they are wearing the same yellow dress all four days of the conference, you never know why they are acting crazy with getting all types of roommates, you never know. So be nice and welcome people when they show up; life is hard, and you never know what people are hiding behind their smile or their scowl.

I am going to explain the yellow dress. On January 9, 2017 I started a weight loss/fitness competition with Gold's Gym. I was a size XL, 163 pounds, depressed, stressed and totally ignoring that taking care of my self is the yestokindness thing to do.

My sisters invited me to start going to the gym in June 2016, to which I said yes, and then I created the sauna, steam room, hot tub routine: 10-minute steam room, 15-minute sauna, 15-minute hot tub, and if I was feeling extra motivated I would swim two laps (there and back) or ride the lazy bike for a mile or two.

I loved going with them, and I loved that they didn't pressure me or make me feel crappy for being different than they were. I call this the pre-workout workout: six months of getting in the habit of going to the gym. One day I even sat in the locker room paying my bills and the daycare lady came in and we laughed and she said she didn't care what I did while I was here as long as I was in the building.

Just show up. Just go to the gym. You have to preappreciate yourself by paying it forward to yourself at the gym. You need yourself and your body and your mind and your soul if you are going to do the most good on this earth. One is not without the other. So start now. Look, people can change. If I can change, you can change too.

Long story short, I won the competition. I got a trainer, Chance Hadley, who rocked my socks off and pushed me farther than I thought I could go, and I won. I got a check for $1,000 and a two-year membership to Gold's Gym.

Sometimes I am writing thinking, what the heck am I talking about and why does this have to do with anything…oh, the dress. So I wore the yellow dress every day that week because I lost so many inches I went from a size XL to medium in just twelve weeks. I couldn't afford to get new clothes before I went. So, I'm just saying you never know, you don't see the person washing their yellow dress in their bathtub so it's clean the next day. You don't see the cereal they packed, or the struggle, or the giants they have to face when they get home. You see the smile. Unless they choose to be bitter, then you see the scowl. We always get to choose. I choose smile, what do you choose?

I met two of my new favorite people there, and we became a MasterKind group. If it weren't for them and our calls, this book wouldn't even be a reality. Seriously, some day you will see our trio on stage, or you can just hire us: me, Randy Fox (foxpoint.net) and Bennie Lambert. (BennieLambert.com). We have been cheering each other on, helping each other focus, and soon will create a power-house trio. And that is the benefit of showing up when it's probably safer not to. That is the benefit of taking a risk and putting yourself around people who can make a difference in your life. Get out of bed. You can do this.

As I am writing this book, I am on a flight to Amsterdam, by myself, on Halloween. Good thing I got my mom guilt in check. I'm connecting to Rwanda and Uganda, Africa. I'm going to Africa, by myself. That is an entirely different book. Preorder now on my web-site. LOL, again not joking; it's a good one.

I'm watching *License to Wed*, a movie with Robin Williams in it. So in case you quit reading now because you're offended by my swearing or lack of grammatical aptitude, let me be clear: the main point of this book is to remind *you* that *you* matter. You, yes you, the one reading this or listening to it, the one who has struggles that I know nothing about, the struggles that you hide behind your smile, or scowl. No matter what you have done or haven't done, or choices you have made, people you have hurt along the way, you can change. You can be different tomorrow or at least in twenty-one days.

You got this.

Reach up. Reach out. Ask for help from someone who can or will help you. It's not too late.

You are not a lost cause. You are not too far gone.

Please, do not kill yourself slowly or otherwise. Put down the bottle, the pills, the gun; step back off the ledge and listen to me when I say, I have been there. I have been there so many times, and that is why I can go to Africa by myself because I am not afraid of anything that anyone can do to me, because I have hurt myself so bad. I have hated myself more than anyone ever could. I have begged to die. I have tried in many ways to be done, and I am still here. There is a reason that I am still here, and there is a reason that you are here. Who knows, maybe someday you will be the one who saves my life. We all need each other, we all go up and down and around. We need us.

So stay.

Stay with me here, join me in making the world #safetobehuman.

Okay, back to the association chapter. Wow, people, if this book actually gets published and into your hands, then it proves that anyone can do anything.

I know there is a force that wants to stop good—whatever you call it, I know you know what I'm talking about. It's the force that makes doing good so hard, it's the force that makes you want to kill yourself right before you end up giving the speech of your life that actually ends up saving someone else's life. I know this because the words we say have power to save. I have sat in an audience where Kathy Helou, National Sales Director of Mary Kay, saved my life with her words. I have given a speech where someone came up and said, "I struggle with that too. Your words really spoke to me today, thanks for sharing."

It's that force that distracts you with a million good things, so you can't focus and do the one true good you were meant here to do. It's the forces that have kept this book in my head and in my notebook for so long; it doesn't want us to inspire each other. Fear is contagious, and it can spread like wildfire, and so is bravery, so when someone is being brave it ruins their plan. Fear. Insecurity, complaining, the depressive state is where this force likes us to be.

Preappreciation has the power in the darkest of times to remind people that the good they do matters, that their efforts to provide a space or a message matters. The struggle is real, and if you don't know what I'm talking about then you haven't taken the time to get real and go deep and really see why you are here and what purpose you are here to fulfill. We all have unique beautiful things to do while we are here, or we can be lame and do nothing. That is our choice too; free agency, free will is the gift to all.

Let's use our free will to inspire, uplift, and love each other. Let love be the saving grace I'll say it again, and I'll say it a million times: You never know what people are hiding behind their smile or their scowl. As business leaders, community leaders and fellow human kind, what else is our purpose if not to make life easier for others?

Over the years I have had many responses to the thousands of cards that I have sent out. These responses range from anything to no response at all, to an e-mail back, a card back, or even a phone call. Darryl Davis a best-selling real estate author (darrylda-visseminars.com) will always call me whenever I send him a card. Of course, I have never answered because I used to have phone-answering-a-phobia. When we got to the Influence 2016 in Arizona, Darryl sat down with me and helped me with a few things; that definitely wouldn't have happened if we hadn't already made a connection before the event.

What do we live for, if not to make life less difficult for each other?
—George Eliot

One time I sent a card to this guy in Germany. He received the card and searched me out on Facebook and thanked me for the card. When I went to the next national meeting, I found him and said, "Hey! I'm the girl who sent you the postcard." He looked at me a little blank stare-ish; it was super awkward, probably too much time had passed, so I learned quickly not to confront people about if they had received the card. These things work better if I just let them flow. I didn't completely stop; sometimes my curiosity got the best of me and I would ask people, but it never ended well.

I got an e-mail once from a friend who is subscribed to an e-mail list of a lady I had sent a card to, and she had written in her blog about getting a card from me, but I never would have known if I didn't have the friend who looped it back to me. This is the thing, we have to do better at spreading good gossip. If you hear something good about someone, loop it back to them. We need to hear more often that the good we do matters, that we have made a difference in someone's life.

I know that people say that we should just do good with no thought of reward, but it gets old. Doing good is, at times, damn hard, it gets dark and lonely, it's not all sunshine and rainbows! We who want to do good need to team up together and cheer each other on.

This morning, my dad called me and told me that he met a friend of mine, and she told him that I had saved her life. I called him to get the details. She was ready to end it all, and she watched my post about kindness and suicide awareness and she is still here today. I had no idea, and this is a high-functioning, high-profile, high-impact person. I'm serious, this crap works, and if we took the time to spread the good we do and the good others do, and stop spreading dirty gossip, I'm sure we could change the world around pretty darn quick.

It always cracks me up when people say, "I don't want to brag" right before they are about to share something amazing they did for someone else. But when it comes to gossip, we tend to spread it around without pausing to see if anyone wants to hear it without thinking about the consequences. Stop apologizing for sharing good and start pausing before you spread gossip. Apply the THINK Model:

THINK
T-Is it true?
H-Is it helpful?
I-Is it inspiring?
N-Is it necessary?
K-Is it kind?

I love this, maybe I'm going to sell phone cases with this printed on the back, so that people can remember that the words they say matter. You can't take back the pain your words cause; even if you apologize it doesn't make it like it never happened. Especially when you are mad, pause, zip your lips, maybe try texting yourself something that you want to send others and see how it feels receiving it.

The truth is you never know what people are going to face that day, and you want your words to uplift and inspire, life is too hard to be beating people up for every little thing. It's good, we're good, life is good. We're all just human…let's make it #safetobehuman.

I try—emphasis on try—to no longer attach myself to what comes of the cards I send or the good I do. I honestly used to feel bad if there was no response or acknowledgment, but I (try to) no longer hope for it. I am just surprised and grateful if I do hear something back. Karmically enough they always come back at the perfect time, on my darkest days; they are the light that helps me through.

This truly is the joy of it all, that what you send out literally comes back.

CHAPTER SEVEN

. . . .

Preappreciation in Your Community

One of my favorite stories of the importance of preappreciation was when I sent my stepdaughter's teacher and principal a thank-you in advance before the school year started. I had to do some research to find out who it was, and lo and behold her principal in her fifth grade year of school was none other than my fifth grade teacher Mr. Reese! He was one of my favorite, most memorable teachers, and I would never have known or made the connection if I hadn't researched it and sent that at the beginning of the year. This will create connections in the beginning when they can do the most good.

This year, as my kids are in school I randomly send thank-you notes just to say thank you. Teachers have to have the hardest jobs in the world, so thank them, and thank them often. Please don't wait until teacher appreciation day. I'm giving you permission to do it earlier, and more often. Even if it's just a Post-it note in your child's folder...do not over complicate it! Just do it!

My friend Amy—she is basically the bomb dot com—I met in Rotary; we have done a few service projects together. She is one of those humans who does so much good for everyone all of the time. I know you know one, or you are one, whoever it is that you know— hug them, let them know it matters. So, I gave Amy a stack of my #preappreciation cards and she flipped through the phone book and randomly, anonymously, sent them to doctors or business people cheering them on, encouraging them. I almost cried when she told me that; on the hardest of days, our days can be brighter by simply looking out and seeing who else might need to be uplifted. We all struggle, we all act like we don't struggle. If we could just somehow remember that the same thoughts and feelings that you have, I have as well. We all have the exact same different struggles, let's just uplift and encourage instead of pointing out what's wrong and critiquing all of the time. Pause, try it: send a note to someone random. If you don't have a card lying around or a flash card, then cut a paper about envelope size and send a piece of paper. It doesn't matter if it's not perfect, just send out good.

When I first started I didn't let tacky stop me, I sent out hundreds and hundreds of flash-card notes. Bright pink, yellow, orange, and green, when I finally got my website www.yestokindness.com I got a stamp, a high-class stamp, and added that to my brightly colored flashcards. I'm just saying, don't try to make things look perfect and then never do it. As the old proverb says, the pathway to hell is paved with good intentions. Stop thinking, planning, scheming, just do it, do something, do something right now. Put down this book, it's not more important than the people in your life, send something now. It matters.

Another thing that I have tried, and this helps a lot with phone calls to doctors, insurance, banks, businesses, anywhere that you are on hold for literally seventeen hours and then you have to traverse the fake recorded lady that can never understand what you're trying to say so by the time you actually get to a live person you are already upset, pissed off, and not ready to talk nice. If companies think about it, they are setting themselves up for failure! So! This is how we change it on our end, our baseline has got to change. Instead of having an attitude of "I'm the customer," "I'm bugged," "I'm inconvenienced," "I'm, I'm, I'm." If we want to make the world #safetobehuman, then we have to leave a trail of goodness behind us. We have so much power, and preappreciation can help us literally leave a trail of sunshine behind us, leaving everyone we meet along the way in a better, more uplifted state.

So, when the real person answers, first step is smile, just smile. Even though you're bugged, force yourself to smile.

Second step, remember that you never know what life challenge that person is facing and a mean, upset, annoyed, high-maintenance phone call could be a tipping point. Remember that your annoyed tone transcends phone waves, and so can your smile. It is an easy switch if you pause to think about it. Be that person that people talk about because they love you, you inspire them to be better. The world is full of critics and people who point out everything that is wrong, be the person to find the good. Another good thing you could do is to write thank you notes while you're on hold! It's hard to be mad while you are sending out gratitude!

Another way to preappreciate is to leave a good review. Even though it happens after, it's the time that is taken and it helps others on their search for good business. On that note, commit to always finding the good in every company and leaving that comment. So…I try to leave reviews often and even if it wasn't a perfect experience I try to find one good thing they did.

Well, this one time we went to a motel in California. I don't know what was going on there, but the entire world must have been in LA because every hotel was booked for miles. We finally found a sketchy hotel: one king bed, five of us. I was trying to be grateful, but it was really hard. I'm not going to go into detail about the things wrong with the place, but let's just say it was rough. Well, we left the worst review, detailed, specific, and completely discouraging. We got a phone call a few days later, we had left all five of our passports on the top of the fridge. The owner mailed them to us. I felt so horrible. I wished I could take back the review, I wished I could unsay the truth. The truth was, it was a place for us to stay, the people were nice; it was a motel, not a Hilton. We paid a fair price, it was the last available hotel because of our failure to plan. I have never left a bad review since this time. My stomach is gut wrenched even as I write this. I'm not asking you to lie on a review or give a fake good review. I'm asking you to find the good and share that. Share the good. Look for the good. Find the good. Be the good. Leave a trail of light and goodness behind you. There are enough critics.

Plug for doing good and volunteering: people say they don't have time or energy for it, but I promise you will meet the most amazing people and build friendships that last a lifetime. Commit to do more good, even if it's just saying yes one more time a week, it matters. Things don't just happen, events take a lot of people and many hands make light work.

CHAPTER EIGHT

. . . .

Drive Kind

I am always thinking of situations where I can use preappreciation, and one day I was driving and thought, using a blinker is a nice way to preappreciate someone while driving. Try it, even though it's a law, some people forget how to do it. So, I'll explain how it works. If you are in the left lane, and you want to get over to the right, you put your blinker on first: this informs everyone around you of your intent. You then look in the mirrors and check your blind spot, and if it's safe you move over. Where I am from in Utah they don't even use blinkers, it's like a big surprise! I'm getting over! I know why they do this though, they do it because as soon as a driver in Utah sees a blinker, they speed up and get in that driver's blind spot—"Oh no, you don't. You're not getting over." So, if you see someone put their blinker on, then the courteous thing to do is to tap on your breaks and let them get over. It's not a race and no one is going to the same place.

Doesn't it just make you feel all warm and fuzzy inside when someone cuts you off to speed ahead and then is stopped by the same red light in three seconds? People, we have to do better at making the roads safe to be human on.

You never know what is going on in someone's vehicle or why they are acting the way they are. One day, I was driving in Sardine Canyon, it's the road you have to go through to get to Logan, Utah—it is beautiful. When I got to the top of the canyon and started head-ing down, my car shut off. I had no idea what was wrong with it. I couldn't think straight, and I didn't know what to do. I knew there was a gas station at the bottom, so I stayed in the fast lane so I could turn left. I was going slow, in the fast lane, in Utah. Cars were driving by me honking, pointing, telling me to move over. It was so stressful, not just that my car was broken down, but that my life was broken down. I had things going on that I can't even write on these pages because it will burst into flames. I had things going on in my mind that I would surely go right to hell for. I was barely making it, and to top it off my car gave out too. I remember thinking that you never know why people are driving slowly in the fast lane of life, you never know why someone is acting crazy or rude or selfish. Maybe they're in survival mode? Maybe they can't breathe because they have so much going on. Did you know that when you're in panic mode, you literally cannot think? You go into fight or flight mode and anything that is not vital shuts off. So when you are on the outside looking in, you have all the answers that are so simple. Remember that you are not in the same state of mind as the person in the middle of the firefight. Easy for you to say is such a valid response because if you are in the state of mind to see the solution, then you have no idea what it feels like to be in the state of the mind of the problem. That is why we need each other. So, if you offer a suggestion do it in a loving way, not in a judgmental kind of a way.

I got to the gas station okay, and I got help with the car. I can't even remember what was wrong with it, I just remember that it took an entire gallon of antifreeze and that the guy who helped me was hot.

Life is not a race, the same car you cut off and flip off will be the same car you are sitting next to at the stoplight twenty meters ahead. Slow down. Smile while you drive, tap on your breaks, and let someone in. Don't drive slow in the fast lane. Oh, my gosh, that is why I love living in the east, people move over. If you pull up behind someone in the fast lane, they move over, it's the most amazing thing. In Utah they slow down, and then when there is a chance to go around them, they speed up. Chill! Put in a good song and instead of being mad at everyone—just wonder—wonder why they are the way they are and breathe. You're going to get there. It's all going to be okay.

Preappreciate each other on the road by driving kindly. Slow down, leave time to get where you need to go, smile, look at other vehicles like they are on the same team with the same goal of getting home to our families at night.

For the longest time, I could never put my business on my vehicle. You know how people have their phone number in their window, I never ever did this because I had such road rage that I couldn't drive and advertise.

One time before cell phones were illegal to operate while driving, I was in the fast lane headed to Logan and someone in front of me was driving so slowly. I pulled out my phone to call them to tell them to move over, but someone called me at the same time. I never got to have that conversation, but I wonder how it would have gone.

"Hello."

"Hi, I'm in the vehicle behind you, could you please get out of the fast lane if you are going to continue to drive so slow?"

I mean seriously, these are the things that go on in my head while I'm driving.

So many people spend so much time in their vehicle. Here are a few things we can do to make it more manageable for everyone.

1. Have a "we're on the same team" mindset. Remember that everyone is headed somewhere, dealing with hard things that we know nothing about.

2. Turn your radio to KLove. It's such a nice station with uplifting music. It is the gateway drug to Jesus, so if you're not into that then definitely don't start because Jesus will get in your soul if you listen to it. If you have too much money at the end of the month you could always donate to their ministry at www.klove.com. Thanks, KLove, for your role in my life of kindness.

3. Relax, slow down, smile, and breathe. The journey is as important as the destination. If you get there fast but leave a trail of destruction behind you then what is the point. Leave a trail of goodness behind you. It matters. You matter.

CHAPTER NINE

· ·

Using Preappreciation at Home

A simple way to preappreciate your family is to prep the night before for the next day. It is really hard to be a good human when you're overstressed and last minute all of the time. Our kids both started school this year. They were born 10 Months and 28 days apart, and the school year cutoff is different here in NY, so they could go to kindergarten and first grade a year earlier than if we lived in Utah. So, we went from no kids in school to both kids in school. Every night, well, most every night we lay out their clothes on a chair with shoes, socks, hats, scarves, boots, gloves, backpacks so everything is ready to go. If we happen to sleep in or have a hard morning, then I am always grateful to know that all of that is set out ready, waiting for us.

I even have started laying out my clothes for the next day, it takes one less thing off my plate that morning. In all this good we do, we must not to forget to include ourselves in it. When I started exercising this was an essential part of working out, laying out my workout clothes the night before. I promise, try this: have it all in a pile, ready to go, then it's one less obstacle you have to overcome. If you wake up and your shorts are in the washer and your shoes are outside with mud on the bottom then it's just too easy to say screw it, I'll work out tomorrow. We have one body, one mind, one soul, today is all we have. There is no tomorrow for thousands of people every day and we never know when we will lose our ability to take care of ourselves, so do it now.

This also includes things like projects that are due tomorrow: make sure they're done the night before. For Girl Scouts, I always make sure my copies are made and my projects are ready by Tuesday night because who knows what Wednesday brings. Make it easy on yourself, preappreciate yourself by prepping the night before for the next day.

My sister taught me this cool thing about how to preappreciate your body. If you think about it our bodies are amazing, and most of us treat them like crap. Imagine if we treated our cars the way we treated our bodies, many of us would be broken down on the side of the road.

Besides the obvious but extremely challenging ways you know like, ummm, eating vegetables and drinking enough water, there is a thing you can do every time you take a shower. You start at the top of your head—and this is quick so it doesn't waste too much water—but you basically tell your entire body thank you for all you're going to do today. Thank you, head, for protecting my brain; thank you, brain, for all the good thoughts we are going to have today; thank you, eyes, for seeing the good; thank you, mouth, for saying uplifting things; thank you, ears, for the gift of hearing; thank you, neck, for keeping my head on; thank you, shoulders, for carrying the burdens of the day; thank you, arms, for being strong; thank you, hands, for all the good you will do today; thank you, veins, blood, heart, for staying soft; thank you, stomach, for finding your flat; thank you, organs, liver, lungs, kidneys, reproductive system, bum, legs, and feet, for all you will do today. Thank you, bones, muscles, and skin, for protecting me and reminding me to be strong on the inside and soft on the outside. (Insert your name here) body, thank you for all you are going to do today, thank you for showing up and making the world a better place. It matters, you matter. Let's do this!

I would be lying if I say I did that every day, but I do it often and I think of my sister every time, so sorry if you think of me now every time you shower—awkward! Think of all the good you can do with your body that you have given some time to preappreciate.

Another way to preappreciate at home is to give a fifteen-minute warning before you get home. Often my husband will call and say

"I'll be home soon" so this gives me time to put down my Facebook, turn off Grey's Anatomy (just kidding, I only watch this Thursday night while I'm folding laundry) and act like I have been cleaning and cooking all day. It is just nice not to be surprised. It's nice to have warning to change from mom alone at home having peace and quiet to wife and mother mode. Speaking of Grey's Anatomy, check out the TED talk that Shonda Rhimes did on "My Year of Saying Yes to Everything". It has changed how I look at parenting and the time I have with my littles. Here is the Link (https://youtu.be/gmj-azFbpkA).

Even at dinner we have a deal that whoever cooked, the other person cleans up with the kids. So if I cooked, while we are eating I will say to my husband, thank you in advance for cleaning up. He started this and I love it because I get my thank-you before doing the thankless jobs that need to be done. Its way better to already have a thank-you in the bag than to wonder if anyone even notices, cares, or appreciates all the things there are to do at home.

If you are a mom, this is me thanking you in advance for all the good you will do, all the times you clean the house and it ends up looking worse than when you started. All the late nights and early mornings, the tears, the puke, the Band-Aids, the whining, the bedtimes that seem like jail time would be easier. You got this. You are doing more good than you know. You are doing better than you think. Keep going, put down the Delta app and don't buy that one-way trip to Tahiti. Your kids need you, stay, it matters. You matter.

CHAPTER TEN

. . . .

Preappreciate Yourself

I was at the gym during that business trip in Florida, the one I went on instead of paying all my bills that month. I saw my new friend there, Cam Calkoen. He is an international speaker from New Zealand. He is amazing! Check out his website at camcalkoen.com. We had met a few days before, I had shown up early and volunteered to greet people. The lady in charge had told me to save myself some seats up front. I saved two on the front row, and then I saved two a few rows back for some reason. When Cam and his friend walked through the door, I knew I liked them right away. I asked if they would like a seat up front and ushered them up there. They were both very grateful, and I am so grateful to know them.

While in the gym, Cam said something that will stay with me forever. He said, "Going to the gym is paying it forward for yourself." I loved that! I try to do all this good as much as I can, and for the past five or six years I have let go of taking care of myself, and his words helped me see how important it is to pay it forward...for ourselves. Preappreciating ourselves by going to the gym is a gift we give ourselves, then we have already "put on our own mask" so we can go out and do good.

The truth is we have One Body. One Mind. One Soul. We need all of those to live life to the fullest. If we spend all our time expanding the mind and lose our body, our lives will be less than they can be. If we spend all our time on our soul and have a beautiful soul but let our mind and body go…what do we have? It takes all three, everyday something… I don't care what you have chosen in the past, you can change.

I first heard about this body, mind soul stuff from a book written in 1910, by Wallace D. Wattles. "The Science of Getting Rich" He also says that more than charity and pity, the world needs You, and many other good people to get as rich as possible. Getting rich, is the best thing you can do for the world. Buy this book- It's a life changer! Thank you Jen Sincero for introducing me to this book, in your amazing book, "You are a Bad-Ass at Making Money". You can download that on the Audible App, or get it off her website. (www.jensincero.com)

If you would have known me from 2011–2016 you wouldn't even recognize me. For all of those years, I look back through my pictures and there are literally *none*. No pictures of me with my kids, or selfies, or anything like that. I was a medium in my mind, so seeing the pictures of myself were just too much to handle. It started small, just going to the gym, watching free YouTube workout videos, walking around the neighborhood. I promise, if you want to change, there is a way. If you don't have money or motivation or anything, you can still change. It's 2018: anyone who wants to change, can. You will have to ask for help, and you will have to do things that make you uncomfortable, but seriously. YOU CAN DO THIS! Here is a list of friends who have businesses that can help you. I'm serious, you can do it!

Taylor Stroud www.isagenix.com/taylorstroud
Kristy Sunday www.isagenix.com/kristysunday
Dan Rawls www.eatbetterwithjuiceplus.com

Chance Hadley is the best personal trainer ever. He is not accepting new clients at this time…when he is, I will let you know! Life changer!

It's okay to ask for help. It's okay to pay people to help you; they have families to feed and dreams to achieve just as you do. It's a combo of decreasing stress, increasing appreciation, increasing water intake, increasing veggie intake, and sometimes you need a boost with a supplement. During my Gold's Gym Challenge, I always thought in terms of adding in the good instead of diet or lack. Like in dieting and life, add in so much good that you are *full* of it and it seeps out your soul! What you fill your heart and mind and body with affects how you treat yourself and others! Choose. Live in choice. Live in abundance.

Meditation is another beautiful way to preappreciate yourself. I promise. I know all y'all have heard of it, and tried it, or never tried it. I finally, finally found a way that works for me to do it, and maybe it will work for you too. There is an app, it's called Calm. This book is starting to feel like a glorified sales pitch for all my friends, but I'm just sharing what works for me, and I promise, if you do what works for others you'll find that it sometimes works for you too. If not, then you keep trying until you find your thing. That is why life is so beautiful and why we all need all of us, some people will read this book and not even finish it because they can't stand how I write, or how I look, or the fact that I go to the bathroom with the door open (I don't like to be boxed in). It doesn't matter, nothing matters, if you wake up in the morning with anything good to do, then you will probably offend someone or get criticized by someone, but do it anyway! Get up, do good, repeat. At times those who complain the most do the least, there will always be those people. Plan on it. Prepare for it, know that when it happens you are on the right track.

Back to Calm. The reason that I love this app the most is because it tracks the days you meditate and says things like "Good job, you're on a 12 day streak." Then it has a calendar with stickers over the days you did meditate. Secondly, the meditations are ten minutes, so it's easy to add into my day. Also, there are categories of different meditation options, so if you're having a hard time sleeping there is a deep sleep meditation, or one to calm anxiety, happiness, gratitude, and many, many more. I love it, I use it. It also has a reminder that will go off to remind you to meditate!

I started on June 28, 2017 and currently I am on a fifteen-day streak. My longest streak is sixteen days. I have spent 57 hours, 49 minutes and a total of 298 sessions. I share this because there is so much power in tracking, and looking back over the months, it is good to see progress. The creators at Calm have done a really amazing job. I paid for my yearly subscription in full. They also have monthly plans. Now that I have an app myself, I realize how much work it takes, and I am gladly willing to pay for apps where before I would not.

Just in writing this I found out that they are launching the Calm Classroom Initiative. They are offering teachers all over the world free access to Calm. The Dalai Lama said, "If every eight-year-old in the world is taught meditation, we will eliminate violence from the world within one generation."

Can you imagine, our world where our children know how to quiet their mind, pause, and make a better choice? If you think about the state of our world right now, it's easy to blame God or the government or the churches or the schools or even the families…blaming will do nothing but cause more malice and strife.

If we could find a way to calm our own hearts it would ripple out to our families, then loved and cherished people would go out in the world and wave to their neighbors and smile and drive nicely, then people at work could do better because their customers were nicer, then the communities would be stronger because the businesses would be doing better. The communities would be united and create a stronger state, which would create a united nation, translated out to a world where it is #safetobehuman.

I'm not talking about sunshine and rainbows because I know life is not that way. I'm talking about you and me makes two; we commit to making our hearts calm and our minds clear. We change, increase our vibration, and others notice, and want to do the same.

For an entire year I spoke about ideas to be kind, while destroying my body and soul with an addiction that I struggle with to this day. I still haven't kicked it, but I also haven't given up either. You see, you never know what people are hiding behind their smile or their scowl. If you have an addiction you are hiding, please reach out and get help. People can change, you can change. I can change. It's scary to do good and still struggle with addiction. It's scary to be human and get out of bed. It's scary to have a burning in my soul to do good when I haven't perfected all of my issues.

I want you to look at me and say, hey, I'm better than that. If she can do it, so can I. I want to stand here in front of you, flaws and all, so that you can see that you don't have to have it all together to make a difference. You don't have to be perfect to do good. Sometimes you don't have the luxury of a round-trip ticket, you have to buy a one-way and trust that somehow you will get back to where you need to be.

Since I moved to New York in March I have flown to Utah several times on a one-way ticket. While I am there I bust my butt and hustle so that I can buy a ticket home. When I went to Africa, I bought a one-way ticket. I needed the universe to know I was serious about going. I'm asking you to buy a one-way ticket for your life and then work your ass off for a trip home. We don't always have tomorrow. Give good goodbyes and leave a trail of goodness behind you. You never know when you will have to backtrack and end up stepping in your own crap.

One last quick idea on preappreciating yourself: I started listening to motivational YouTube videos when I work out or in the morning when I can't get out of bed or on the off chance that I find myself cleaning. I'm just saying, our minds can quickly turn into a scary place to be, if you start every day off with a dump load of positivity it gives your day a much better chance. Set the tone of your day to be blessed, to be kind, to be good. Here is a link to my favorite YouTube video: https://youtu.be/5diEq1gTE4Y. In this one, Denzel Washington even talks about saying thank you in advance! This is such exciting stuff!

CHAPTER ELEVEN

. . . .

Opportunities Will Come

The first year I went to Influence in 2015, I had joined the National Speakers Association just a few weeks before, and I knew that I had to go. If you don't do anything different from reading this book, please start showing up. Show up when it doesn't make sense, show up when you have better things to do, show up when you're tired, show up late, and even when you don't feel like it. Looking back, showing up has made the biggest difference in my life.

So my Dad and I go this this event, my friend lived in DC so the plan was to stay at her house. It was only, ya know...like two hours away! We showed up and at the airport we met two people who took us under their wing and helped us get from SLC to DC; we were like lost puppies, I swear. Steve Weber was one of them, he ended up becoming a great friend and accountability partner. This guy is the most consistent person that I know. He puts out a daily inspiration, you gotta sign up for his e-mails. I love them and look forward to them. Go to www.speakinggump.com seriously, pause, subscribe!

This is totally taking me on a tangent, but I subscribe to everyone. If there is a place to put my e-mail I do it. I used to be selective, but one day it hit me, subscribing to people's e-mails gives me options. Of course I do not read all of them, nor do I delete all of them, but randomly exactly what I need comes through those e-mails, which I wouldn't have gotten if I hadn't been subscribed. If you don't want to subscribe to everyone, then at least subscribe to your friends, let's support each other. Right now, set this book down (I think that is the most repeated line in my entire book!) pause, and post this on Facebook!

Subscription request! Who has an e-mail list I can subscribe to? I want to support you and your business! Post below!

This is not a hoopla of good intentions; we have to stop thinking and talking, we have to got to get into the flow and take inspired action. When an idea comes into our head, do it. When someone pops into our heads, text them, e-mail them or get on my app and send them a handwritten card. I'm not even going to tell you to put the book down to download my app, but it is on Apple Products search (pre thank you). I used pre thank you instead of preappreciation because I thought it was easier to spell! I crack myself up. If you have an idea for an app or need one for your business, my app guy is the best! Send him an e-mail at chris@contenta.io. He is an app genius, a fabulous renter, and I'm happy to call him my friend. Thank you, Chris.

Show up! When you have an idea, do something right now—there is no later, there is no tomorrow. All the energy we waste worrying about tomorrow we could be doing so much good!

Okay, so back to Influence 2015, so Steve and Mitch Seehusen (www.mitchseehusen.com) were very kind, and let us share a shuttle to the hotel where the conference was held, the exact same hotel that we did not have a reservation for. My dad went up to the front desk, very nicely dressed with his American flag tie, he asked them if they had a room. They said they had a room for the night, but only that night. Every day for four days he went down to the front desk and kindly asked them if we could have the room for one more night. We got a room every time. We overheard one of the top speakers complaining in the lobby because he didn't get a room, but my dad did. Kindness matters. Being gracious matters, people will help you if you leave your overinflated entitled self at the door and treat people with kindness and graciousness. It matters, people matter.

While I was there, I got to spend some special time with my dad. Growing up with ten kids we never really got one-on-one time.

I was proud to be there with him. One day we were in the elevator and this guy from our state got on the elevator with us. He said something to my dad that hurt my feelings, and when he got out I asked my dad why he was so nice to him when he was such a jerk. My dad replied, "How he treats me says nothing about me, it only says something about him." As we walked away, I told my dad that I would hold his grudge for him. I wasn't satisfied with him letting it go so easily. I told him that he wasn't holding the grudge properly, so I would hold it for him. Luckily, he helped me let that go too; life is too short to hold your own grudges, let alone someone else's. Please don't follow people around picking up their grudges; if they don't care enough to keep them, then you can let them go too. My dad is an amazing speaker with a big heart to do good, my dad teaches me every day how to be a good person, check out his website at www.douglasjdickson.com.

During one of the sessions, I got to hear from Mark Scharenbroich. I hope the whole world gets a chance to hear him speak in person. He has this way of connecting and making you feel like you matter, the way he holds the audience in his hands is nothing short of magical. When we got home, his speech was mailed out with the monthly magazine. I watched it over and over again, I even made my kids listen to it as punishment. I laughed, I cried, and then I sent him a thank-you note. Okay, truth be told, I didn't send him just one, I sent him lots of ones. I sent him so many that he sent me one back, with a gift card to Costa Vida. Some people call this stalking, but I call it perseverance.

The next year in Arizona at Influence 2016 I got to meet him. As soon as I got up to him and introduced myself, he got pulled away. I was crushed for like one second, but then I talked myself down. I smiled and walked away thinking, *it's okay, I'm okay.* Well, guess what, Mark came back, he found me and he said thank you for all the cards and to keep sending them. He came back. I will never forget.

If you have people who look up to you, go back, remember what it was like to be the little guy and treat them like they matter.

Like Mark did. Go back. Find the people who look up to you, and let them know you care.

That same year, Influence 2016, I forgot my name tag so I was headed back to my room to get it. I see this lady running to the elevator; I tried to put my foot in the door but it was too late. I pushed the open button over and over so she could make it on the elevator. She was so grateful, she asked me what I spoke about. My usual reply was kindness, but for some reason I started telling her about how I had sent cards out to say thank-you in advance to all of the speakers. She loved the idea. She had never heard it before. She told me she was a radio host in Canada and asked if I could be on her show. Stephanie was the first person who gave light to my idea; she saw it and helped me see that it was a valuable message. I pray everyone can have a Stephanie Staples in their life. I hope everyone has a person that lets them see that their message is powerful and good and must be shared. The people we need and who need us are all around us; unplug, look up, smile, be kind, do some good, and find your perfect people. If you wonder what your message is, then start shining light on other people's message until you find yours. Find Stephanie at www.yourlifeunlimited.ca.

CHAPTER TWELVE

. . . .

Beginning of a New End

I like to believe that one person can make a difference, and the power in sharing our goodness goes on and on. For me, and see if you agree, I think that inspiration is cyclical: at one point you may inspire someone and light their fire and their flame will likely be the one to rekindle your fire when your dark days come, as they surely will. It's not like you inspire someone and then will always be ahead or above them. You go up and down and around; you are enlightened by the same person who will someday let you down. Your life may be saved someday by the same person who you once looked down upon.

Even in the past few days struggle arises with writing a book. I had sent out a preappreciation card to Tammy Anderson Ward, an amazing speaker and coach who puts on events to provide a space for other people to share their message. On the day when I was wrestling with *what's the point of doing good, people are so mean*, she sent me a messenger message that said, "I got your postcards. Thank you so much. I put them where I can see them all of the time." I promise, the good you do will come back when you need it the most. When you are about to rationalize yourself out of your own life, it will be there for you. Find Tammy Anderson Ward at <u>hopehavenevets.net.</u>

The only real truth that matters is that we are all equal. I'll say it again, *we are all equal.* My friend Kimberly Giles (claritypointcoaching.com) made my world stop spinning the day I sat in a room and she said, "We are all equal, our value is exactly

the same, and there is nothing we can do to increase or decrease it."
I had never thought of life this way; I had always put people above
me because they were wealthier or wiser or spoke better. I put people below me because they chose to sin differently than I did, and I
judged them as less good…less effective…less awesome…essentially
worth less than me. Wow, super sucks to admit that on paper, but it's
true. I went around putting people on pedestals and putting myself
on pedestals at times, it's all so exhausting. What if we just let go of the
judgment and wagering of people's value. What if we just agree that
we are all equal? We all matter. It matters that we are where we are.

Life isn't black and white. We have to stop trying to label everything and everyone, so we can function. Let's just be nice, want to?
It's like we label ourselves and then spend the rest of our life trying to
fit in that self-imposed limiting label…

We can't even compare or judge ourselves. You know you have
those days where you are super effective, and then comes a day where
you do absolutely nothing. Then we spiral, we think *what the hell is
wrong with me*? How can I be so effective some days and such a piece
other days? There are so many factors, and we don't even know the
story of our own life, or why we are the way we are, because we screw
it up with judgment and excuses.

Think about the moon, it never compares itself to anyone-es-
pecially to itself. I just lights up the dark! Waxing and waning every
phase in between totally bright to not there at all. Even when it looks
like it's completely gone, it is actually a new moon. Sometimes we
feel like we can light the world on fire with the flame inside of us, and
some days we feel completely gone, it's all okay. Relax, let your good
today be good enough, and let go of comparison. It's okay.

Even right now as I write this I'm judging my husband for playing
Nintendo like it's his second job. He's almost forty, and I'm over here
doing good, changing the world, trying to make us money so we can
turn the heat up. We live in upstate New York for hell's sakes…not sure
why the Dish Network and Netflix gets priority and the heat is the thing
that gets cut from the budget. Oh well, it turns him on. No one is nagging him, he is accomplishing something that makes him feel happy. So
screw me and my judgment. I probably am actually jealous that he can

tune out my nagging, the kids, the messy house, the freezing cold house, and just do what he wants to do. We all could take a lesson from that.

We can't compare our strengths to other people's weaknesses. We can't compare how we decide to spend time, we can't compare or judge how people spend money. All we can do is be nice. We can't control most things in life, but we can control how and when we show our appreciation.

Gratitude. Appreciation. Thankfulness has the power to keep us in the present as we cannot do anything about the past, and worrying about the future is like saying a prayer for what you do not want. Wrap all things in gratitude. It's not a thing to put on your to-do list, it's a way of life. People can feel if you appreciate them, and they want to be around you more the more you appreciate their efforts.

Putting the "pre" in appreciation has the power to turn a common transaction into a real human connection.

Our world has become so transactional; we look at people as money or sex or a how-can-I-use-you-for-my-benefit mentality. We have lost the art of connection because we don't pause to appreciate; we leave it to the end, or we don't do it at all.

This may be because we are stuck in the past replaying it over and over, or because our anxiety for the future wipes us out, or even the possibility of a connection because we aren't even present enough to see a connection if it slaps us in the face.

Come with me on this journey. Join me in reminding people that it matters that they are still here. Because it does. It matters that you are still here.

As my book end thank you—please accept this affirmation as my gift to you.

> I am at the perfect place
> At the perfect time
> With the perfect people
> Until we meet again, you got this;

Tammy joy

ABOUT THE AUTHOR

Tammy is an Iraq War veteran and was diagnosed with PTSD and bipolar disorder. Tammy has survived multiple suicide attempts and in 2015 she founded yestokindness.com with the mission to eradicate suicide through random acts of kindness. Tammy is a Tedx speaker and an appreciation coach—she loves teaching others that gratitude closes the gap between where we are and where we want to be. She loves to play softball and really, really, really just wants to do good for a living. Tammy was born in Utah, the fifth child of ten kids. She currently lives in California with her husband and three amazing daughters.